Britisches Freikorps

British Volunteers
of the
Waffen-SS
1943-1945

Richard Landwehr

SIEGRUNEN MONOGRAPH 6
BENNINGTON, VERMONT
2012

First Edition published in 1992 by Richard Landwehr, Jr.
Second Revised Edition published in 2008 by Merriam Press

Third Edition (2012)

ISBN 978-1475059243
Merriam Press SR6-P

This work was designed, produced, and published in
the United States of America by the

Merriam Press
133 Elm Street Suite 3R
Bennington VT 05201

E-mail: ray@merriam-press.com
Web site: merriam-press.com

The Merriam Press publishes new manuscripts on historical subjects, especially military history and with an emphasis on World War II, as well as reprinting previously published works, including reports, documents, manuals, articles and other materials on historical topics.

Rear Cover
A member of the British Free Corps (Britisches Freikorps) of the Waffen-SS. (Erik Rundkvist)

Contents

Dedication

*This title is respectfully dedicated to
the members of the
British Free Corps
of the Waffen-SS,
living or dead.*

Preface

THE story of the British volunteers of the Waffen-SS has long been treated with scorn and derision by the "establishment" media. After all there weren't many of them and their small unit, the British Free Corps, was somewhat comic-opera in nature. This publication at least will try and change that perception. The hard core nucleus of the BFC consisted of serious, committed individuals who deeply believed in what they were doing and stayed on until the end. Therefore they deserve to be treated with respect; they were a part, however minuscule, of the vast Pan-European Army that was the Waffen-SS and no one can take that away from them. In future generations that fact will be treated as a true badge of honor.

The BFC was an effort to navigate "uncharted waters"; no one in the Waffen-SS was quite sure if it was possible or even "legal" to recruit POWs from an active belligerent to use as soldiers of the German Armed Forces, albeit even though their service was to be directed against the Soviet Bolsheviks. That meant that the whole undertaking to recruit British and other Allied soldiers was a tentative one and was never developed as fully as it possibly could have been. The post-war British socialist government made it clear that the Free Corpsmen were to be treated as traitors by executing the founder of the BFC and bringing the rest to trial. They were, in modern day vernacular, "political criminals" or "prisoners of conscience".

The story of the British volunteers of the Waffen-SS was however a unique and honorable one—if it can be divorced from the travesty of British domestic politics—and it deserves telling in a fair minded manner, which I indeed hope this work can accomplish!

Chapter 1

The Legion of St. George

THE concept of a British volunteer military force fighting alongside Germany against Soviet Bolshevism, seems to have originally been developed by John Amery, the son of a British cabinet minister and a POW with a pronounced anti-communist viewpoint. After choosing to do propaganda work for the Germans, Amery came up with the idea of the Legion of St. George, an organization to be comprised of militarily unfit English internees who would conduct pro-NS publicity rallies throughout German occupied Europe. Amery had his plan approved by both the German Foreign Ministry in Berlin and the OKW (Wehrmacht High Command) in February 1943, with the proviso that the Legion of St. George would instead be a combat unit, similar to the Germanic Legions serving with the Waffen-SS. Permission was granted to recruit up to 1500 internees/POWs for the unit.

On 21 April 1943, the first efforts at recruiting for the Legion of St. George were carried out at a British POW camp in France. Prominent British collaborators made speeches to the assembled POWs and conducted interviews throughout the following week with prospective enlistees. At the time, John Amery was still in charge of the operation. In order to facilitate his original proposal for a non-combatant propaganda unit, he created the British Anti-Bolshevik League as an offshoot of the Legion. The first volunteer for the Anti-Bolshevik League turned out to be a pacifist English professor, while the first two recruits for the Legion were Maurice Tumnor, (a Briton of French ancestry) and Edward Jordan, a POW who had already been collaborating a little too closely with the Germans for some of his former comrades; i.e. they considered him a "stool pigeon".

A number of other British volunteers soon signed up, but there was also one important defector: John Amery. Amery resigned from his leadership position with the Legion and the League by citing "personal problems" and his inability to equip the Legion with British uniforms. However his actions were not sufficient to save him from the gallows once the victorious Allies got their hands on him in 1945! In May 1943, Adolf Hitler supposedly decided to place a special emphasis on encouraging recruits for the Legion. The idea of a British volunteer unit seems to have appealed to him, as it was one that he had been contemplating himself for over a year previously.

As part of the new recruiting procedures, former BUF (British Union of Fascists) members and known anti-communists were to be segregated from the other POWs and sent to their own special indoctrination camp. Special Detachment 999 was set up to attract "Commonwealth" officers who might at least be willing to join the Anti-Bolshevik League. But the detachment was not highly successful, garnering but 6 recruits before it was terminated at the end of September 1943. The Legion of St. George itself was also struggling, having obtained only 11 members by June 1943. Therefore the Special Detachment 517 was established in Berlin to help gain some more personnel.

Some 270 POWs, deemed likely prospects for the Legion, were sent to a special "rest" camp administered by Special Detachment 517. From this group, 20 quickly signed up and were sent together to the Genshagen Barracks. A command structure was set up and five British Army and Royal Air Force NCOs were selected to run the unit. Overall command was given to a Quartermaster Sergeant "Owen", assisted by a Sergeant "Trinder" (disciplinary NCO), a Sergeant "Dixon" (senior medical orderly), and two RAF bombardiers. The British Legionnaires were treated with a special deference by the Germans, and were permitted to take "field trips" and outings to areas of interest, such as historic Potsdam and the National Olympic Stadium.

One of the principal recruiters for the Legion was Corporal Thomas Halle (or Haller) Cooper, an Anglo-German, (German mother, English father), who had adopted German citizenship prior to the war and had served in combat with the famous "Leibstandarte SS Adolf Hitler" of the Waffen-SS, (the Legion

10

itself was not yet firmly affiliated with that organization). As an experiment, groups of POWs selected by Special Detachment 517 were sent to live with the Legion members at the Genshagen Barracks. After a certain period of time these POWs were given the option of either enlisting or returning to a POW camp. Most chose the latter option, although a number of recruits were gained in this manner for the Legion. Among the newcomers were a Sergeant-Major "Montgomery" of the Commandos, (who would serve with the unit until the end), a Sergeant-Major "Taylor" of the Hampshire Regiment and a small number of Canadians and merchant seamen.

By the end of August 1943, the Legion of the St. George contained almost 50 members, most of whom were interested in joining the Waffen-SS and serving with their Germanic comrades on the Eastern Front. The early Legion volunteers enjoyed a great deal of personal freedom and some were even allowed to live by themselves in Berlin, even while still wearing their British Army uniforms! This caused some problems for the Legionnaires "Edward Jordan" and "Walter Plauen". During the night of 22/23 November 1943, they went out into the streets of Berlin to try and help clean up some debris from an Allied air raid while dressed in their old uniforms. This did not go unnoticed by some of the civilians and the two Britons were quickly arrested by an SA man on civil defense duty who delivered them to the Gestapo headquarters on Prinz Albrechtstrasse. It took six hours to clear the matter up and the incident actually made the back pages of a Swedish newspaper!

From the summer of 1943 on the British volunteer unit came under the overall jurisdiction of the SS Hauptamt (SS Main Office), specifically Department D-I, otherwise known as the Germanischen Leitstelle or Germanic Central Administration. This office was concerned with supervising the affairs of the "Germanic SS" within the Waffen-SS and ran an "inspectorate" of Germanic Offices, and a political leadership school, (the "Germanic House" in Hildesheim, later in Hannover). It came under the command of the Swiss SS-Obersturmbannführer (Lt.Col.) Dr. Franz Riedwig, (born 10 April 1907/SS Nr.

293,744), who had formerly been a medical officer with the SS Division "Viking". In October 1943, Ostubaf. Dr. Riedwig found himself suddenly transferred into the III.SS Panzer Korps (Germanic), where he again resumed his medical duties.

In the course of that month he had given a speech at the SS-Junkerschule Tölz advocating far greater autonomy for the German occupied countries in Europe which Reichsführer-SS Himmler felt was inappropriate. However a year later, much of what Riedwig was promoting became the official policy (on paper at least), of the Waffen-SS. Ostubaf. Dr. Riedwig's replacement as head of the Germanischen Leitstelle was SS-Standartenführer (Col.) Erich Spaarman, (Born 19 July 1907/SS Nr. 1,752).

In addition to the Germanischen Leitstelle, Department D of the SS Main Office also contained Department D-II, which was responsible for the political Germanic-SS. This office was directed by SS-Ostubaf. Max Kopischke, (born 26 March 1899/SS Nr. 229,652), a former instructor at SS-JS Tölz. This department had two sections (D-II la and D-II lb), which dealt with the Germanic SS in Germany (la) and in other countries (lb). Germanic political SS volunteers from Flanders, Holland, Denmark, Switzerland, Norway, Liechtenstein and elsewhere were handled by these sections. These volunteers were not necessarily members of the Waffen-SS, although many of them were. In charge of Section DII la was SS-Untersturmführer (2nd Lt.) Johannes Gustke. British recruits were primarily dealt with by Department D-I, and many would be attached to the "Germanic House" program directed by SS-Stubaf. Paulsen.

It is relevant to detail the functions of the SS Hauptamt, as listed in the guidebook issued to members of the Waffen-SS of all nationalities in 1944: "The task of the SS Hauptamt is to create a close communal Order. It is responsible therefore for the selection of men suitable for the Schützstaffel and the registration of SS members and their families; and in addition for the philosophic and political direction, education and training of the whole SS and Police, as well as for the welfare of mobilized units of the SS and Police, (Troops Welfare). A further task is the physical training and the pre- and post-military training of the SS. Of particular importance is the selection, organization and direction of the SS in the Germanic countries and the propagation of the Germanic idea in all spheres of life."

Chapter 2

The Britisches Freikorps

ON 1 January 1944 the Legion of St. George officially became the Britisches Freikorps of the Waffen-SS, or in its English translation, the British Free Corps, which was abbreviated as the BFC. This followed the decision by the unit NCOs to request full combat-capable status for the British volunteers, which in turn granted them access to Waffen-SS training facilities. A resolution had therefore been drawn up and sent to Adolf Hitler requesting the change in unit status and title. It read as follows:

"We the true soldiers of Britain, wish to swear allegiance to the Fuehrer and the German Reich. We volunteer to fight side by side with the Germans to beat the enemies of Europe. For this purpose, we the undersigned, make application for a corps to be called the British Free Corps."

The proposal was promptly accepted by Adolf Hitler, and immediately thereafter, the Waffen-SS took full responsibility for the British volunteers. The Britons had been under Waffen-SS control all along, but until now it had been on a more-or-less probationary basis. Since the previous summer, the officer in charge of the British volunteer unit had been SS-Hauptsturmführer Hans Roepke, (born 14 May 1916/SS Nr. 347,048), a former officer in the "Viking" SS Division, who had lost an arm in combat. Roepke is referred to as "Johannes Roggenfeld" in the book about the BFC entitled *Yeomen of Valhalla* by Marquis de Slade. It was one of a number of names altered by that author, which makes it somewhat difficult to identify all of the real personalities in the book. In any case, Hans Roepke's identity had already been revealed in a previously published work, *Die Waffen-SS, Eine Dokumentation* by Dr. K.-G. Klietmann. For the record it should be noted that all of the British volunteers of the Waffen-SS enlisted under assumed identities for their own protection and only in a few cases are the actual names known. Hopefully in those instances it will no longer be dangerous to reveal the identities.

In late 1943, the Legion camp in Berlin was known as Stalag III D, a reminder that the British volunteers were still regarded basically as POWs. However the billets were soon shifted to a guesthouse in the Pankow district, which along with a nearby cafe had been requisitioned for the exclusive use of the Legion. Recruiting was still being carried out in POW camps at least via the distribution of "free passes" and assorted leaflets that promised special treatment to volunteers. These brought scores of prospects but few takers.

A number of Irish volunteers also served in the German Armed Forces and according to some sources they were used to pose as British volunteers for the purpose of domestic propaganda. The so-called "Irish Brigade", outfitted in black cast-off SS uniforms with SS insignia and Union Jack armshields, supposedly moved from town-to-town throughout Germany to give the impression to civilians that a large number of "Britons" had joined up to serve with the forces of the Reich. Up to 400 Irishmen were alleged to have participated, but this is pretty much unverifiable. Scattered Irish volunteers did serve in the Waffen-SS through the end of the war, primarily in Otto Skorzeny's SS Jagdverbände commandos and in the "Dirlewanger" disciplinary units. However most of the Irish who came to Germany were repatriated via Portugal prior to the conclusion of hostilities.

Unbeknownst to him, the Legion of St. George had adopted the abdicated King Edward VIII, (the Duke of Windsor), as their "patron". He was considered pro-German and possibly mildly pro-NS, and his portrait appeared in the Legion quarters. Most of the hardcore members of the Legion were strong National Socialists, who regretted that Adolf Hitler had not been born in Britain! By the end of 1943, several Australians, New Zealanders and Canadians had joined the Britons in the Legion. In addition to Hstuf. Roepke, a number of other English-speaking Germans were loosely attached to the Legion; notable among them was a

China-born German, "Wilhelm Reisner" (real name—Wilhelm Roessler), who was known simply as "Bob" to the Legionnaires.

While some members of the Legion/BFC still preferred to wear British-style uniforms, most members of the contingent figured that this would not only be impractical, but would (as had already been demonstrated), subject them to possible arrest when out in public. Thus Waffen-SS "Feldgrau" uniforms were adopted without much difficulty immediately after the proposal to form the BFC was accepted by the Fuehrer. For insignia, the BFC was eventually issued a Union Jack armshield in the Waffen-SS pattern along with a cuff-title bearing the lettering BRITISCHES FREIKORPS. A collar patch displaying the three prone lions of the British crest was also issued; this came in silver on red and silver on black formats, a subject that will be discussed in more detail later on. The BFC also had its own flag: a black banner with a small Union Jack in the upper left corner and the initials "BFC" in gold thread in the lower right corner. Most of this unit insignia came into being in the spring of 1944.

In early 1944, some British volunteers put in a request to the Waffen-SS for an officer of their own nationality to command the BFC, but this was not possible as no British officer had yet volunteered for the unit. The Englishmen were now being treated seriously though and an effort was made to streamline BFC operations. A waiver was granted to the Free Corpsmen allowing them to forego the otherwise obligatory Waffen-SS blood-type tattoo, since this was seen as too "incriminating" should the volunteers again fall into the hands of some of their less-understanding fellow countrymen. The BFC itself was formed into a compact 30 man platoon for training purposed under the British NCOs "Bartlet", "Milton", "Montgomery", "Regan", "Wood" and Cooper. A number of border-line volunteers were now released from service, while still others were transferred to Waffen-SS combat units.

Several Britons were sent to the SS Training and Replacement Battalion 3 of the 3rd SS Panzer Division "Totenkopf" in early 1944. Prior to the advent of the BFC, there had been a group of British volunteers scattered through some "Totenkopf" units. In point of fact, a Waffen-SS manpower report issued on 4 May 1940 showed 5 British volunteers serving in the SS "Totenkopf" Division and 2 more in the SS "Totenkopf" Standarten, (i.e. independent "Deathshead" Regiments that were soon mostly incorporated into other Waffen-SS formations). Virtually nothing is known about the "Totenkopf" Britons, but it can be safely presumed that their identities were well concealed to prevent post-war reprisals.

Hstuf. Roepke was not the only candidate in the running to be the permanent commander of the BFC; a Sturmbannführer from the "Viking" Division who came from the Netherlands Antilles and spoke fluent English was also considered for the post but in the final analysis was passed over.

In February 1944, the non-coms of the BFC were dispatched on recruiting tours of various POW camps. The only non-participant in this effort was SS-Scharführer Thomas Cooper, who re-donned his "LAH" uniform to join the war correspondents of SS Regiment "Kurt Eggers" on the Eastern Front. During the latter part of January 1944, Hstuf. Roepke inspected the BFC billets in Pankow and afterwards turned in a report on the status of the unit to the head of the SS Hauptamt, SS-Obergruppenführer Gottlob Berger. Berger in turn briefed Reichsführer-SS Himmler on the developments in the BFC. This led to the release of a three-part declaration by the RF-SS concerning the BFC on 30 January 1944. The contents of the declaration went as follows:

1) All anti-Bolsheviks were to be separated from the general British POW population for the purpose of enlisting them in a new force to fight against the Soviets. They were never to be used against their own countrymen.

2) All British volunteers in the Waffen-SS would be guaranteed the same postwar benefits to be granted to their German counterparts.

3) SS-Ogruf. Berger of the SS Hauptamt was to issue a monthly progress report on the BFC.

On 10 February 1944, the BFC was transferred from Pankow to the "Leibstandarte SS Adolf Hitler" barracks at Lichterfelde in the southern part of Berlin. Here they were joined by SS-Scharführer Butcher and five other BFC members who had been serving as "observers" on the Eastern Front with the "Kurt Eggers" Regiment. Most of the "observers" were obviously demoralized and proved unable to offer any favorable comments on what they had seen and experienced. This caused two of the Free Corpsman to desert and turn themselves in to the nearest POW camp. It was clear that the deteriorating military situation in the east had a negative impact on the morale of some of the English volunteers at least.

By this time the BFC had been fully transferred to the operational control of Branch D-l of the SS Hauptamt, which was now under the direction of Ostubaf. Erich Spaarman. Spaarman decided to try and give the BFC its own British commander. He managed to get a civilian propaganda figure, "Vivian Stranders", commissioned an SS-Sturmbannführer with the hope that he might be made the head of the BFC. For this reason, Hstuf. Roepke was designated as only the "temporary officer commanding". However Stubaf. "Stranders" proved to be a washout without any interest in military service per se.

Late in February 1944, Ostubaf. Spaarman decided to transfer the whole BFC to the "Germanic House" at Hildesheim in Hannover to mold it into a more ideologically cohesive unit. The "Germanic House" was part of a large former monastic complex that now serviced the political needs of SS personnel from various European nations. Upon arrival at the Hildesheim railroad station, Hstuf. Roepke met with his troops and gave them a spirited address in English, indicating that once the BFC had obtained enough new members it would be sent on directly to the Germanic SS Volunteer Training Camp at Sennheim in Alsace for combat instruction. After settling in at the "Germanic House" the first official clerical registration of the British Waffen-SS enlistments took place and the volunteers received a new distribution of uniform items, including SS belt buckles, ties and boots.

At the end of March 1944, a pair of "Commonwealth" volunteers who had been serving as truck drivers with the Flak Detachment of the 1st SS Panzer Division "LAH", turned up at the BFC quarters under the escort of a German "LAH" member. The two, James Conen, a taxi-driver from London, and William J. Celliers, a policeman from South West Africa, had been POWs in Italy. After the coup against Mussolini, they had been permitted to escape by their Italian captors and in a group of about 30 in all, tried to make their way to Switzerland. However at the same time, (mid-September 1943), the 1st SS Panzer Division was in the area of northern Italy where the escape took place, and the Flak Detachment from the division sent out some motorcycle squads to try and round up the escapees. This was accomplished without too much difficulty, but the two POWs mentioned above very adamantly expressed their unwillingness to return to captivity. One thing led to another and they soon volunteered to serve as "Hiwis", (Hilfswilligen or voluntary helpers), with the "LAH" Flak Detachment.

The Flak Detachment commander, SS-Stubaf. Hugo Ullerich, was short of truck drivers and since the two "Commonwealth" volunteers had experience in that area, they were sworn in as "Hiwis" and given trucks to drive. One of the two drove the cook wagon for the unit during its next stint in Russia in the autumn and winter of 1943-44. In March 1944, when the "LAH" was scheduled to be transferred to Western Europe, the two "Commonwealth" volunteers were sent to the BFC to see if they could be induced into joining up. During their service with the 1st SS Division, they had worn Waffen-SS uniforms without insignia, but had also kept their old British Army uniforms on hand, packed and available.

Both of these men had been decorated with the Iron Cross, 2nd Class, and were technically on "leave" along with their German SS escort. After their arrival at the BFC quarters in the "Germanic House", the two were interviewed by a German-American SS officer who spoke fluent English. Their escort from the "LAH" was startled by the whole scenario. He found the BFC billets to be an astonishingly disorderly "recreation hall", very much non-German in its overall demeanor! But by the same token it was also a real paradise compared to the normal Waffen-SS accommodations. Despite being given the "hard sell" neither Conen or Celliers signed up for duty with the BFC. They next spent some time working for the SS Hauptamt and the garrison commander in Fuerstenwalde-Bad Saarow, one of them serving as a driver and the other as an orderly. An effort was made to get them back to the "LAH" Flak Detachment but this was forbidden by higher authorities and their further fate is unknown. A detailed account of the service of William Celliers and James Conen with the "Leibstandarte SS Adolf Hitler" can be found in the book *Gefaehrten Unsrer Jugend: Die Flak-Abteilung Der Leibstandarte* (Verlag K.W. Schuetz KG, 1984).

While at the "Germanic House", the BFC members were required to tender their resignations from the British Army and sign a modest loyalty statement which took the place of the usual oath of allegiance made to Adolf Hitler by most Waffen-SS volunteers. The statement read as follows:

> I (name of the volunteer), being a British subject, consider it my duty to offer my services in the common European struggle against Communism, and hereby apply to enlist in the British Free Corps.

This statement was printed in English (not German) on a form that was signed by the volunteer and then filed away. After this was accomplished the BFC members all received pay books and became eligible for the standard benefits given to Waffen-SS members of whatever nationality.

At about this time, "Bob", the China-born German chaperon for the BFC, applied for a transfer from the Wehrmacht into the Waffen-SS so that he could continue to serve with the English SS unit. Recruiting still remained the primary occupation for members of the Free Corps, and many of them continued to make the rounds of about 40 different POW camps trying to find some new volunteers. On some of these trips the British SS men would be accompanied by an American Army Air Force officer from

Texas. This individual soon applied for combat duty with the Waffen-SS and was listed as missing-in-action in March 1945. His true identity has never been ascertained, but he was one of several individual American citizens to serve in the Waffen-SS, all of whom were given extra protection as far as identification went.

During the spring of 1944, a special effort was made to gain BFC recruits from among 270 pro-National Socialist South African POWs who had been kept segregated from their fellows. Even given their sympathies for the Germans, few of them were willing to commit to what increasingly looked like a lost cause. From this batch, only 3 members eventually joined the BFC. In sum total, the Spring 1944 recruiting campaign netted 10 more volunteers for the BFC. However it must be noted that senior British officers at many of the POW camps had very effectively stopped the BFC propaganda efforts and had forbidden any of the POWs in their "care" from signing on, equating such an action with "treason".

With the campaign in Italy now in full swing, a special recruiting leaflet was prepared to hopefully lure frontline British Army soldiers to come over to the other side. The text of this document read as follows:

Fellow Countrymen! We of the British Free Corps are fighting for you ! We are fighting with the best of Europe's youth to preserve our European civilization from the menace of Jewish Communism. MAKE NO MISTAKE ABOUT IT! Europe includes England. Should Soviet Russia ever overcome Germany and the other European countries fighting with her, nothing on this earth would save the continent from Communism, and our own country would inevitably sooner or later succumb. We are British. We love England and all it stands for. Most of us have fought on the battlefields of France, of Libya, Greece or Italy, and many of our best comrades are lying there—sacrificed in this war of Jewish revenge. We felt then we were being lied to and betrayed. Now we know it for certain. This conflict between England and

Germany is racial SUICIDE. We must unite and take up arms against the common enemy. We ask you to come into our ranks and fight shoulder to shoulder with us for Europe and England!! (Published by the British Free Corps).

Chapter 3

The BFC in Training

ON 1 April 1944, the BFC members were issued new uniforms which included Waffen-SS style ski caps and surplus greatcoats. In addition a new Britisches Freikorps cuff title in silver Gothic lettering on a black field was introduced, (it was later replaced by one with the same wording but in block letters).

From this time on a training schedule was followed at the Haus Germanian (Germanic House), and sidearms, (without ammunition), were issued to the BFC NCOs. Rifle drills and live firing practices were still not permitted. However the Free Corpsmen went through a daily routine of exercises that began each morning at 08:00 with an inspection parade. This was a formal affair conducted by the senior sergeants. Each parade was ended with the German salute and a rousing chorus of "Heil Hitler!" from all of the participants. Afterwards a daily report on the condition of the BFC was submitted to Hstuf. Roepke. In the afternoon hours, the British SS men marched in formation through Hildesheim either en route to the local swimming pool or the soccer field for sports recreation. The Waffen-SS was a big believer in the virtues of athletic endeavors!

On 20 April 1944, two recruits were accused of mutiny and were subsequently dismissed from the Corps. Because of their (unspecified) actions, Hstuf. Roepke decided to discipline his entire command, and he made the other Corpsmen drill for the entire day, which being the Führer's birthday, would otherwise have probably been a "holiday". At this time a request was made from the ranks to relocate the Union Jack armshield on the right coat sleeve to a position above the German national emblem (eagle and swastika). Hstuf. Roepke approved the proposal and passed it on to his superiors in the SS Hauptamt who most emphatically rejected the idea!

In May 1944, the BFC added an English Captain from a Scottish Regiment in the hopes of at last having a legitimate British officer. Unfortunately nobody checked out the Captain's mental condition and he soon proved to be not altogether responsive; in fact he was somewhat demented and was quickly released from service. Hstuf. Roepke assigned SS-Scharführers Cooper and McCarthy the task of returning the Captain to his former POW camp. They were not enamored with the job and just deposited him at the nearest railroad station, leaving him to fare for himself. Hopefully he reached his destination!

A rumor now developed that some of the BFC recruiting teams that made the rounds of the POW camps had been deliberately rejecting applicants to the Corps on the grounds that they themselves might lose their own somewhat privileged positions. No one could verify this, but it seems rather unlikely to have taken place. At any rate, recruiting efforts were becoming increasingly futile as Germany's military fortunes began to diminish. This led to the issuance of another BFC recruiting flyer in the spring of 1944:

As a result of repeated applications from British subjects from all parts of the world wishing to take part in the common European struggle against Bolshevism, authorization has recently been given for the creation of a British volunteer unit. The British Free Corps publishes herewith the following short statement of the aims and principals of the unit.

1. The BFC is a thoroughly British volunteer unit conceived and created by British subjects from all parts of the Empire who have taken up arms and pledged their lives in the common European struggle against Soviet Russia.

2. The BFC condemns the war with Germany and the sacrifice of British blood in the interests of Jewry and international Finance, and regards this conflict as a

fundamental betrayal of the British People and British Imperial interests.

3. The BFC desires the establishment of peace in Europe, the development of close friendly relations between England and Germany, and the encouragement of mutual understanding and collaboration between the two great Germanic peoples.

4. The BFC will neither make war against Britain or the British Crown, nor support any action or policy detrimental to the interests of the British people. Published by the British Free Corps. C1433.

This leaflet was soon being distributed in the POW camps, however the senior POW officers in every camp posted notices that anyone joining up with the BFC would be guilty of committing an act of "treason". Nonetheless, recruits continued to trickle in to the BFC, but usually only enough to make up for losses due to desertions and expulsions. In 1944, the BFC fluctuated between 30 and 50 members, some of whom were on detached service elsewhere. The successful invasion of Normandy by the Allies helped to terminate the broad based BFC recruitment endeavors in the POW camps. There was an increasing fear that the Allies would not look kindly upon those who were perpetrating these activities should they happen to catch them, which looked like an increasingly good possibility.

From the summer of 1944 onwards, the BFC recruitment program was tightened up; only "good" prospects were actively solicited and they had to undergo a very tight psychological, medical and ideological screening process. There was no longer any room for unstable personalities or possible infiltrators. Anyone serving from now on had to be absolutely trustworthy and competent. As the summer progressed, Hstuf. Roepke and the British liaison officer to the SS Hauptamt, Stubaf. "Stranders", both proposed that the privileged propaganda status for the British volunteers should be ended and that the BFC should be integrated into a Waffen-SS combat unit. This proposal would soon be accepted by the SS-Hauptamt.

During the summer of 1944, BFC members began serving as rescue and clean-up workers following numerous Allied bombing attacks in the Hildesheim-Hannover area, but otherwise the general status of the Corps had not changed appreciably. For patriotic reasons five of the British volunteers now chose to place their Union Jack armshields on their right uniform sleeves above the German national emblem, (eagle and swastika), violating Waffen-SS regulations in the process. Hstuf. Roepke noticed this breach of the rules and he attempted, calmly at first, to try and get the volunteers to rescind their somewhat defiant actions. However they refused to do so, so Roepke was forced to take disciplinary measures. Two of the Britons were expelled from the BFC and the other three were given several weeks at hard labor. In response to the "acting commander's" actions, two more of the British volunteers chose to permanently transfer into the "Kurt Eggers" SS War Reporters Regiment, while several others sought direct release from service.

For a brief time the BFC was actually threatened with dissolution but the crisis passed due to several new occurrences. For one thing, Hstuf. Roepke apparently was given an indefinite leave of absence, (records are vague on this point), by Branch D-1 of the SS Hauptamt and he was supposedly replaced by a one-legged English speaking SS-Hauptsturmführer from the 2nd SS Panzer Division "Das Reich". Also the three Britons who had been assigned to work details due to the "insignia incident" were brought back and reinstated in the Corps and a very popular half-English medical orderly from the 9th SS Panzer Division "Hohenstaufen" transferred into the BFC. All of this resulted in an increase in morale and a return to normalcy, but it is safe to say that official uniform regulations were never flaunted again!

On 4 September 1944, the BFC began relocating to the Waffen-SS training area near Dresden in Wehrkreis IV. The unit consisted of 2 Sergeants, 4 Corporals and 21 Privates for a total of 27 personnel in all not counting those on duty with the "Totenkopf" Division or the "Kurt Eggers" Regiment. The BFC was sent by train to the Pionierkaserne (Pioneer Barracks) in Dresden, which was the home of an SS Combat Engineer Training School and Replacement Battalion. Up through 1943 most of the SS divisional engineer battalions had been formed here, but by 1944 the SS Engineer Training School at Hradischko in Bohemia, which had a greater variety of terrain to utilize in maneuvers, had become the major center for Waffen-SS combat engineer (pioneer) training. As a result much of the Dresden facility was being used for the more prosaic pursuit of providing basic training for Waffen-SS recruits. When the BFC appeared on the scene there were approximately 4,000 other Waffen-SS troops at the barracks under the overall supervision of SS-Obersturmbannführer Ferdinand Tietz, (born 19 Dec. 1943/SS Nr. 247,061), who also commanded the SS Engineer Training and Replacement Battalion 1. He was a holder of the Iron Cross, 1st Class.

Upon arriving at its destination, the fully uniformed BFC contingent was drawn up on parade and greeted by the base commander. After inspecting the English volunteers, he gave them a short speech professing his confidence in their abilities and informing them about the many other European volunteers at the facility. The BFC was then marched to its own single-story barracks building which was more than adequate to house the whole unit! The building was soon decorated with the BFC flag and a portrait of the ex-King Edward VIII.

A comprehensive program consisting of language, ideological and infantry-engineer training was then drawn up for the Corps by its commanding officer along with the assistance of Hstuf. "Harry Mehner", a German-American. Towards the end of September, Hstuf. "Mehner" became the acting BFC commander when his superior was forced to take an extended convalescent leave. Basic training was now carried out for the first time in earnest and morale in the unit climbed. It certainly was an improvement over the previous year of largely inactive duty.

The German language lessons given to the volunteers were to a large extent concerned with military terminology so that the Englishmen could function efficiently in a combat situation. Ideological instruction was basic, logical and truthful and dealt with the Pan-European ideal and the international struggle against Plutocrat-Bolshevism. It was not the sinister "brain washing" that has been implied by hate-mongering establishment "historians".

Ideology instructors included Hstuf. "Mehner" and Waffen-SS students from the nearby Martin Luther University who served as guest lecturers.

In October 1944, SS-Standartenführer Gunter d'Alquen, the chief of the SS War Correspondents Regiment "Kurt Eggers", suggested to Ogruf. Berger, (head of the SS Hauptamt), that the BFC had lost its propaganda value and should be disbanded. D'Alquen was concerned about a potential negative Allied reaction to the utilization of POWs as soldiers that might hinder future negotiations. He was overruled however by both Berger and Reichsführer-SS Himmler. In fact, the RF-SS went the extra mile and now assigned the BFC to the control of the III. SS Panzer Corps (Germanic), effective upon completion of training.

Two members of the BFC in Waffen-SS uniforms with full insignia sometime in 1944. Freecorpsman Kenneth Berry (left) and Freecorpsman Alfred Minchin (center).

SS-Mann Eric Pleasants in BFC uniform wearing the triple lion collar patch.

Eric Pleasants depicted at the Vorkuta slave labor camp in the Soviet Union.

Thomas Haller Cooper in postwar British captivity.

The staff of the Germanischen Leitstelle in 1942. Dr. Franz Riedwig is the tall Sturmbannführer (Major) to the right (facing the photo) of the blond woman.

Germanic Waffen-SS recruits, in this case Flemings, being inspected by SS-Hauptsturmführer (Captain) Neuweiler in Brussels, Belgium on 29 January 1943. The SS troops designated as "Germanic" came from Holland, Flanders, Denmark, Iceland, Norway, Sweden, Switzerland, Liechtenstein, Luxembourg and Great Britain, with special exemptions for the Walloons and Finns. They were considered full-fledged SS men and carried the "SS" designation before their ranks. Slav and Eastern and Southern European volunteers were given "equal but separate" status with the "Germanics" and used the "Waffen" designation before their ranks; i.e. Waffen-Untersturmführer.

SS-Obersturmbannführer (Lt. Col.) Dr. Franz Riedwig, the Swiss head of the Germanischen Leitstelle in the SS Hauptamt until October 1943, under whose jurisdiction the Legion of St. George came.

Assorted Waffen-SS European volunteer armshields. Note the BFC Union Jack variations in the top row. (Military History Shop).

Waffen-SS pattern armshield issued to the members of the British Free Corps. A number of design variations existed, including one with "England" across the top. But it appears from photographs that above design was in general use.

The SS-"Totenkopf" Division, home to many British SS volunteers throughout the war, is seen here in a motorized march through France in this previously unpublished photo. The divisional emblem is displayed on the motorcycle sidecar.

The collar patch for British Waffen-SS volunteers, depicting three heraldic lions (left). This was produced and issued in both silver on black and silver on red editions.

Germanic Waffen-SS recruiting posters. These were produced in many languages for display in different countries. The above posters were used in Flanders.

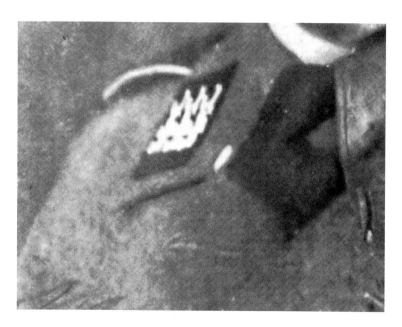

The actual collar patch being worn by a unknown English volunteer.

The cover of an issue of the SS Germanische Leithefte, an inspirational and ideological publication for Germanic SS volunteers. It was produced in several languages. This edition was published in Antwerp in 1942.

Field training with MG 34 light machine guns.

Field training with a motorized vehicle.

The SS athletic suit for sports activities.

In the barracks.

SS-Ostubaf. Ferdinand Tietz (here a Stubaf.), on the left, as commander of the SS Pionierkaserne at Dresden; the home of the BFC in the autumn of 1944, and early winter of 1945.

An oath taking ceremony on the central plaza at the SS Pionierkaserne in Dresden.

A British SS volunteer in walking-out dress that appeared in various European wartime newspapers.

Probably a "re-enactor" (left) in a British Free Corps Waffen-SS camouflage combat uniform. The triple-lion collar patch is visible.

Collar patch of the 11th SS Panzergrenadier Div. "Nordland" (left), worn by some, but not all, members of the division.

An armored "cannon wagon" from the SS Armored Reconnaissance Detachment 11/11th SS Div. "Nordland", to which the BFC was assigned in 1945.

MIA from the "Nordland" Division wearing the "sunwheel" collar patch.

European volunteers from the III. SS Panzer Corps (Germanic) on the Narva Front in Estonia, 1944.

Officers from the "Nordland" Division witness a display of the operation of a light field mortar—a handy "artillery substitute".

Inspection parade—the Hauptsturmführer salutes his men.

Soldiers and vehicles of the SS-Panzer Aufklärungs Abteilung 11 (SS Armored Reconnaissance Detachment 11) of the 11th SS-Frw.Pz.Gr.Div. "Nordland", the unit to which the BFC combat troops were assigned.

A European volunteer from the "Nordland" Division using trench binoculars. He is wearing the "sunwheel" collar patch.

The commander of SS-Panzer Aufklärungs Abteilung 1l/"Nordland", Stubaf. Rudolf Saalbach (center). On the left is the Danish Ustuf. Georg Eriksen, (killed in action), and on the right is the Swedish Ostuf. Hans-Goesta Pehrsson, commander of the 3rd Company in the Detachment, to which most of the British volunteers were posted. Behind him is Ostuf. Siegfried Lorenz the commander of the 1st Company in the unit.

27th SS Div./III. SS Panzer Corps (Germanic) trenches near Greifenhagen on the West Oder, 17 April 1945. The last line of defense!

SS-Brigadeführer Joachim Ziegler (right), commander of the 11th SS Div. "Nordland", shaking hands with SS-Obersturmbannführer von Bockleberg (left), the chief-of-staff of III. SS Panzer Corps (Germanic).

A Germanic Waffen-SS recruiting poster used in Norway showing the banners of Germany, Finland, Norway, Denmark, Holland and Belgium.

SS-Obergruppenführer (shown here as an SS-Gruppenführer), Felix Steiner, commander of III.SS Panzer Corps (Germanic) and the "11th Panzer Army", a "paper" formation.

Britisches Freikorps

The BFC sleeve title.

Fellow-Countrymen!

We of the British Free Corps are fighting for YOU!
We are fighting with the best of Europe's youth to preserve our
European civilisation and our common cultural heritage from the
menace of Jewish Communism.

MAKE NO MISTAKE ABOUT IT! Europe includes England.
Should Soviet Russia ever overcome Germany and the other European countries fighting with her, nothing on this earth would save
the Continent from Communism, and our own country would
inevitably sooner or later succumb.

We are British. We love England and all it stands for. Most of
us have fought on the battlefields of France, of Lybia, Greece, or
Italy, and many of our best comrades in arms are lying there—
sacrificed in this war of Jewish revenge. We felt then we were
being lied to and betrayed. Now we know it for certain.

This conflict between England and Germany is racial SUICIDE.
We must UNITE and take up arms against the common enemy.
We ask you to join with us in our struggle. We ask you to come
into our ranks and fight shoulder to shoulder with us for Europe
and for England.

Published by the British Free Corps.

First and most famous BFC propaganda flyer.

Chapter 4

Preparing for Combat

A
FTER having been admitted to the III. SS Panzer Corps (Germanic) in October 1944, the BFC was given some new insignia. For starters, the British volunteers were now permitted to wear the "Germania" sleeve title, (which was normally only utilized by the members of SS-Pz.Gr.Rgt.9 "Germania" of the 5th SS Panzer Division "Viking"), along with their "Britisches Freikorps" cuff band. Presumably only one or the other could be worn at one time at the discretion of the individual volunteer, as wearing both together would have constituted another violation of Waffen-SS insignia regulations.

In addition to the sleeve title, new armshields displaying a Union Jack surmounted by the title "Great Britain" were issued. But most spectacular of all were the new "dress" collar patches that were distributed to the Corpsmen. These depicted the three royal prone lions in silver thread on a red velvet background and were made for use on both the left and right collars of a "dress uniform". For field dress, the silver lions on black cloth right collar patch and SS rank insignia left collar patch were still used. If there are rarer "collector's items" from the Third Reich era than the BFC "dress" collar patches, they have yet to be reported. These were certainly legitimate pieces, but probably didn't survive the war and as a result were never reproduced by any of the firms that engaged in such enterprises afterwards.

On 4 November 1944, Hstuf. Roepke permanently relinquished command of the BFC to SS-Obersturmführer Dr. Kuehlich, a combat veteran who had been severely wounded in 1941 and 1943 and was subsequently ruled unfit for further frontline service. The BFC gained some more notoriety later in November when a nervous British volunteer, serving on sentry duty at the SS Pionierkaserne main gate discharged his rifle several times, wounding a German Waffen-SS soldier in the process.

However it was decided not to reprimand the sentry for the incident. A more serious transgression took place at the same time when a local Dresden woman reported to the camp commandant that she had been impregnated by one of the Englishmen. The commandant decided that a wedding was in order and thus took place the first and only known "official" SS marriage of a British volunteer.

On 15 December 1944, Ostuf. Dr. Kuehlich temporarily halted unit training activities in order to make another recruiting effort, which again meant that some of the British volunteers had to make the rounds of the POW camps. A special emphasis was placed on enlisting some new members from a group of South African soldiers who had been captured at Arnhem, Holland in September 1944. Three volunteers were eventually netted from this group. A pair of presumably unsupervised BFC soldiers managed to sign up a total of 8 eager New Zealanders, which on the surface appeared to be somewhat of a coup. But on closer inspection these "volunteers" turned out to be Maori tribesmen who disliked the white New Zealand government! Their enlistment was rejected by other members of the BFC on grounds of racial propriety. Whether or not the SS itself ever knew about the attempt to enlist the Maoris into the BFC is open to question; however by this stage of the war certain racial distinctions had been overlooked and a few Eurasians had turned up in French volunteer units of the German Armed Forces. Such was the animosity of the Maori POWs towards their New Zealand rulers at the time that it might well have proved possible to have set up a successful Maori Legion, but that was quite far beyond the scope and purpose of the Pan-European Waffen-SS!

By January 1945, things had returned to normal for the BFC. Training was near completion and the higher Waffen-SS authorities hoped to employ the Britons within a combat unit of the III. SS Panzer Corps (Germanic) as soon as feasible. At this time the battered remnants of the III. SS Panzer Corps were just arriving back in Germany from the Kurland Front in Latvia and had to be sent right back into battle in Pomerania on an emergency basis. The object now was to add the BFC to the III. SS Panzer

Corps just as soon as it, (or most of its elements), could be withdrawn from action for some extended rest and refitting.

January was not without the usual "incident" for the BFC however; this time no fewer than six Free Corpsmen felt that it was the appropriate time to desert and make a run for the approaching Soviet Red Army. They then hoped to gain asylum by passing themselves off as "escaped POWs". All six men were soon picked up in the Sudetenland; four of them were subsequently dismissed from the BFC and sent back to POW camps; one was actually reinstated in the BFC without punishment and the individual determined to be the ring leader of the affair was sentenced to an indeterminate period of "hard labor".

The BFC combat training period was pronounced finished on 12 February 1945 by Ostuf. Dr. Kuehlich. All that remained now as to incorporate the British volunteers into a fighting SS unit. Unfortunately a very tragic interruption soon took place: on the following night the Allies fire bombed the city of Dresden. In what was probably the greatest single wartime atrocity ever committed, up to a quarter of a million (or more) civilians and refugees may have perished in this criminal terror attack which did not adversely affect any military facilities whatsoever, since these were primarily located in the outskirts or the suburbs of the city. But the 1600 acres of Dresden emanating outwards from the city center were absolutely obliterated. To this day the so-called Allied governments involved go to considerable pains to minimize the real impact of the Dresden bombing while still placing great emphasis on "alleged" undocumented "Nazi atrocities". Historical truth will someday correct the situation but for now we are still in a period of time when establishment lies, deceit and hypocrisy persist.

The horror and anger felt by German citizens at the Dresden terror bombing immediately impacted the British Free Corps, whose presence in the area had never been concealed. A number of local people complained to the Waffen-SS base commander about the BFC being located in the vicinity of Dresden, (the SS Pionierkaserne was in the northern suburbs of the city), and they speculated that some of the Britons may have been surreptitiously feeding information to the Royal Air Force. On the basis of those accusations, the BFC was handed over to the SS-Obergruppenführer in command of the Waffen-SS in Wehrkreis IV, (Military District IV), who ordered the entire unit incarcerated until the situation could be clarified.

Ostuf. Dr. Kuehlich was able to come to the immediate aid of his troops and he delivered documents, (logs and daily reports), to the SS Hauptamt that fully exonerated the British volunteers. However it was clear that the Britons would no longer be welcome in the Dresden area, despite the fact that they wore Waffen-SS Feldgrau. At the end of February 1945, after holding a full dress parade at the SS Pionierkaserne, the BFC was shipped by rail back to Berlin for its final disposition.

In the meantime, the BFC liaison office in Berlin had finally acquired the services of a legitimate British Army officer, a Captain "Webster", the scion of a very prominent English family. "Webster" had chosen to enlist in the BFC after witnessing several indiscriminate Allied terror bombings of civilian areas including one which hit the POW camp he had been held in, causing the deaths of several of his friends and comrades. It now seemed possible, that for the first time the BFC could have an English commanding officer.

When the BFC arrived back in Berlin from Dresden, it was sent to new quarters in a former school house in the Pankow District. Here the Corpsmen were met and addressed by Captain "Webster". He gave the English volunteers a very stirring address about the importance of fighting on the Eastern Front. The die had now been cast; the British SS men were going into combat. But once again the Waffen-SS command was uneasy about using Allied personnel in any manner that might have seemed "forced", so on 8 March 1945, Ostuf. Dr. Kuehlich was authorized to give the Britons one final choice: they could either now serve at the front in a European Waffen-SS unit or they could spend the rest of the war in a disciplinary camp. Admittedly it was not much of a choice! All of the current members of the BFC opted for combat duty.

With that final decision out of the way, things now progressed with rapidity. Obergruppenführer Berger from the SS Hauptamt gave the go-ahead to send the Britons into action and they were authorized to receive first class weaponry; every BFC member was given the latest model 44mm automatic rifle. After drawing their weapons on 8 March, the English SS troops were sent to a rifle range where they spent the afternoon familiarizing themselves with the automatic rifles.

At about this time the last British volunteers signed on for service with the BFC, but only one of them, a Scottish POW who had been captured in Greece in 1941, actually arrived in Berlin to join the main contingent. For the others it was just too late. The fact that Europeans of all nationalities were still trying to voluntarily join the Waffen-SS can only be attributed to the highest call of conscience and duty in the face of overwhelming odds. It was not something that "criminals and traitors" would do and it was quite a contrast to the majority of Allied "resistance" helpers, (terrorists!), who only joined up when it was clear that the "Nazis" were losing the war! But as in most wars it was the losers that had to pay the price, even if they held the moral high ground. For the European Waffen-SS the price was a high one indeed: execution, imprisonment, slave labor, deprivation of civil rights and slander and defamation.

At this time, the BFC was split into two sections. One portion, including the leadership office with Stubaf. "Stranders" and Hstuf. "Webster", was transferred to a temporary operational headquarters in Bremen, while the other portion, an eleven man squad under Scharführer "Montgomery", was sent to a training grounds 30 miles to the northwest of Berlin for practice with portable anti-tank weapons. Ostuf. Dr. Kuehlich, still suffering from war wound related health problems, was now sent to an SS hospital in Denmark, and another German acting commander, SS-Hauptsturmführer "D" (actual name not known), took command of the BFC.

Chapter 5

Into Action

O N 15 March 1945, the British squad assigned to anti-tank weapons training finished its agenda and was dispatched to the headquarters of the III. SS Panzer Corps (Germanic) located near Stettin. This squad now consisted of Scharführer "Hodge" and 10 other men; apparently Scharführer "Montgomery" was no longer with this group. It would be the only "coherent" element of the BFC to see combat action. The BFC squad was quartered in some bombed out apartment flats until the III. SS Corps commander, SS-Obergruppenführer Felix Steiner, could figure out what to do with it.

Finally, on 22 March 1945, the squad led by Scharführer "Hodge" was posted to the SS Panzer Aufklärungs Abteilung 11 (SS Armored Reconnaissance Detachment 11)/11. SS-Freiwilligen Panzer Grenadier Division "Nordland", under the command of the highly decorated SS-Sturmbannführer Rudolf Saalbach. The Britons were sent to a company in the detachment that was situated in the small village of Schoeneberg, near the west bank of the Oder River, (it is not to be confused with the larger town of Schoenberg that was situated farther to the west in Mecklenburg).

At Schoeneberg, the British volunteers were put to work on field defenses, which involved, (among other things), digging trenches. It was not very glamorous work, however the troops were allowed to supplement their rations by hunting deer and rabbits in the nearby forest. Soon after arriving in Schoeneberg, the Britons found themselves engaged with the rest of their company in a fierce pitched battle against a Red Army advance element that was attempting to reconnoiter the area. The sudden appearance of the Soviets was a surprise and part of the company was initially overrun, but the Waffen-SS troops soon regrouped and drove the Reds back, but not before some prisoners had been lost to the communists. Among those to fall into Soviet hands was the SS-Mann "Edward Jordan" (or "Kenneth Edwards"—take your pick, both names were used in different sources), a former merchant seaman. Despite statements to the contrary in the savagely anti-BFC book, *A New Kind of Treason* by Rebecca West, there is no evidence that he had been trying to desert to the Reds; he seems to have been a legitimate captive. After the war he was repatriated to England to stand trial for "treason".

In early April 1945, the rest of the BFC with a strength of some 30 men in all, had been gathered together in Bremen. From there these troopers were sent on to Steinhoefel in north-central Germany, where the III. SS Panzer Corps (Germanic) headquarters was located. The Britons arrived there on 6 April 1945 under the leadership of Hstuf. "Webster", who had assumed active field command of the BFC. "Webster" reported directly to the Corps' commander, Ogruf.

Felix Steiner, who was more than a little bemused and astounded by the transfer of the Englishmen to his command! He subsequently inspected the BFC and then, following his usual custom with foreign volunteer troops, shook hands with each member. Afterwards, he conversed with Hstuf. "Webster", who attested to the loyalty and motivation of the British volunteers in the war against Bolshevism. Steiner accepted that part of the argument but he remained skeptical about the appropriateness of utilizing the Britons in a combat role in light of the position the Allied governments might take against such an action. Nonetheless, the British volunteers were assigned to the Armored Recce Detachment of the "Nordland" Division with the instructions that they were to be dispersed throughout the various companies rather than lumped together in a group. This negated the possibility that the Britons could be wiped out en masse in a single battle.

Both Hstuf. "Webster" and Oberscharführer Thomas Cooper remained as liaison personnel with the III. SS Panzer Corps (Germanic) staff. Scharführer "Montgomery" along with eight British volunteers serving under him joined the 3rd ("Swedish") Company/SS-Pz.Aufkl.Abt.11 under the command of the veteran Swedish Ostuf. Hans-Goesta Pehrsson, who had served for several years on the Eastern Front, first with the "Viking" Division and later with the "Nordland" Division. 3rd Company was known as the "Swedish Company" since most of the Swedish volunteers in the division were concentrated there along with many other Scandinavian soldiers. The Britons were able to adapt well to this unit and soon got on very friendly terms with their European comrades. Despite the desperate military situation, the morale of the BFC members, who were finally on duty with one of the best combat units in the German Armed Forces, had never been higher. For the first and only time in the war they were fully integrated into a frontline, fighting SS troop!

On 14 April 1945, the 11th SS Div. "Nordland" was ordered to go to the defense of Berlin; at the same time Ogruf. Steiner decided to retain the British volunteers in Steinhoefel. He had still not made up his mind over the "legality" of the BFC in the eyes of the Allies and it was a question that had kept bothering him despite the many more critical problems that now faced him. Steiner felt that the BFC might indeed constitute a breach of international law since its members had been recruited in POW camps and he certainly did not want to be held responsible to the Allies for the battlefield actions of the Britons or for losses they might sustain in such endeavors. Steiner was under no illusions about the ultimate outcome of the war at this juncture and he felt that he had to save as much as possible his own position and that of some of the more vulnerable groups of European volunteers. He now also issued an edict forbidding the use in combat of a Flemish Hitler Youth Battalion, (average age 15/16), from the 27th SS Volunteer Div. "Langemarck" (Flemish Nr.l). This injunction was ignored however largely due to the close proximity of the enemy, and the Flemish Hitler Jugend Battalion fought with tremendous courage in several desperate engagements. Tragically, many of the Flemish teenagers ended up as MIAs or in Soviet captivity.

The last phase in the history of the BFC was about to begin. Ogruf. Steiner did not want to send any of his troops to Berlin in what he now felt would be a useless sacrifice; but he had no further control over the destiny of the "Nordland" Division. Still he made absolutely certain that the BFC members in III. SS Panzer Corps (Germanic) wouldn't be involved. He had no way of knowing that there were already at least three Britons in Berlin attached either to the almost defunct BFC HQ staff or to the "Kurt Eggers" SS War Reporters Regiment. In addition, the nominal BFC commander, SS-Hstuf. "D" and the unit paymaster, "China Bob Reisner", were also still in the city as part of the BFC staff.

Chapter 6

Final Days of the BFC

AFTER making his decision to remove the British volunteers from the combat zone, Ogruf. Steiner ordered Hstuf. "Webster" to recall the BFC members from the "Nordland" Division and have them assume non-combatant status. To further enforce this edict, Steiner had Red Cross armbands, signifying neutrality, issued to the Britons. The order was not well received by the British volunteers, the last of whom had only just signed on in the first half of March 1945. The Englishmen had just gotten fully adjusted to their combat role with the "Nordland" Division when they found themselves pulled out of the lines.

Shortly afterwards some 30 members of the BFC were assembled together in Steinhoefel and marched on foot to Neusterlitz in Mecklenburg, where the field command passed from Hstuf. "Webster" to SS-Oberscharführer Thomas Cooper. "Webster" was so discouraged by the decision to remove the BFC from the front lines that he promptly resigned from the Waffen-SS and resumed POW status. About a dozen other English volunteers, apart from the 30 listed above, who had been serving as medical orderlies or war reporters, did manage to stay on duty with the "Nordland" Division, the "Indische Legion" and the "Kurt Eggers" Regiment. Since English was widely spoken in the above mentioned "Indian Legion", (composed of Indian POW volunteers), this was probably a good, if illogical place to send some of the Britons. It was illogical in the sense that the members of this Legion belonged to the "Free India" movement and were preparing to fight against the British, although that turn of events never came about.

In late April 1945, the main body of the BFC under Oscha. Cooper began marching on foot towards the Allied lines and an uncertain fate. There was still the vague hope that they would be accepted by the Allies along with other European volunteers as part of a new multi-national anti-communist army. In retrospect this sounds absurd due to the heavy "democratic" support for Bolshevism, but it was the only bit of rope that many members of the Waffen-SS had to hold on to. At one point in their march westwards, the unescorted Britons were ambushed by a German Army patrol who thought the BFC members were possibly Allied saboteurs in German uniforms. The situation was clarified without any bloodshed but from then on the English SS men were accompanied by a small contingent of German soldiers who acted as an escort.

Hstuf. "D", the titular head of the BFC, had remained in Berlin, and after terminating his duties by destroying all of the files pertaining to the British Waffen-SS soldiers, he volunteered his services to the "Nordland" Division once it arrived to help defend the German capital. Hstuf. "D" was later credited with knocking out a Soviet tank during the battle for Berlin. At least one British SS medic serving with the "Nordland" Division in Berlin also took up arms and was credited with a tank kill; however he was badly wounded in the fighting. A number of other British volunteers were involved in combat actions towards the end of the war, but for the most part their fates remain unresolved and their stories probably will never be told.

At the end of April 1945, the main contingent of the BFC was still short of the Allied lines and the decision was made to go "underground". The Britons abandoned their Waffen-SS uniforms and insignia for British POW clothing that they had been careful to bring with them; they would now pass themselves off as escaped POWs—something that was done, with German permission, by many surviving groups of European SS volunteers. This stunt seems to have worked for a number of the BFC members who were able to quickly reintegrate themselves into British society for a short time at least. Others were not as lucky and were handed over to the British military police until their fates could be determined.

For the record, one British volunteer, SS-Scharführer "Regan" of the "Kurt Eggers" War Reporters Regiment actually fell into Allied hands in full BFC uniform. He had been covering the battle for France and had been accompanying Waffen-SS troops retreating through Belgium in August/September 1944. By some accounts he had actually served in combat during this period. In a skirmish with the Belgian "resistance" Scharführer "Regan" was wounded and fell into the hands of these terrorists who eventually turned him over to the Allies. He was therefore luckier than many German Waffen-SS soldiers who were brutally butchered in captivity by these "freedom fighters". One of the specialties of these "Allied Heroes" during this period of time was to ambush undefended German Red Cross convoys and massacre the wounded. Since the terrorists were soon placed in power in Belgium by the Allies they never had to answer for their crimes but instead went after German "collaborators" with murderous savagery.

After going home to Great Britain, many of the English SS volunteers were "safe" until a socialist "Labour" government was elected to power. The minions of this regime immediately launched a "witch hunt" for ex-BFC members and began hauling them to court on "treason" charges, although none of them had intentionally taken up arms against their own country. The founder of the BFC, John Amery, who had become a Spanish citizen while fighting for the Nationalists in the Spanish Civil War, was found guilty of "high treason" and was executed by hanging. Thomas Cooper, who had been a German citizen since before the war, was sentenced to life imprisonment at hard labor plus an additional 25 years for good measure! One can only hope that at some point in time he was released from this Draconian judgment. Most of the other British SS volunteers, including SS-Hauptscharführer "Montgomery" received sentences of 10 years at hard labor. While in prison the comradeship between the BFC members became much stronger than it had even been in wartime; all were convinced that they had been treated unfairly and most were unrepentant. In fact many of the known present day survivors, estimated to number around a dozen by one source, remain National Socialists to this day.

About nine or ten former BFC members, primarily those who at some point recanted their service, received no legal penalties at all. The ex-SS-Hauptsturmführer "Webster" who had angrily resigned from the Waffen-SS when the BFC was removed from its combat role, not only was never punished for his service but he retained his British Army officer's commission! Family influence may have had something to with this since "Webster" had deep roots in the "aristocracy". SS-Obergruppenführer Steiner was taken to Great Britain from his POW camp after the war in an attempt to get him to testify against "Webster" and other BFC members. To his credit, Steiner refused to cooperate with the British authorities in any way, manner or form.

The other "Empire" (or "Commonwealth") volunteers made out somewhat better than their British counterparts. South African volunteers drew only light monetary fines for their actions, while Australians and New Zealanders were forced to serve very short jail sentences. No record whatsoever is known of what happened to the handful of American volunteers that turned up in the Waffen-SS; presumably most were either killed in action or captivity or were able to successfully assume false identities. Given the secrecy in which the U.S. government traditionally cloaks "inconvenient" occurrences it is quite possible that they are still part of the continuing WWII cover-up. Perhaps someday there will be no further need to maintain the myth of the "Good War", and the full story of Allied misdeeds, atrocities and general censorship of events can finally be exposed! Although one could say this is already long overdue!

Chapter 7

Early Germanic Volunteers in the Waffen-SS

AS early as the 1st of May 1940, the Waffen-SS had a number of "Germanic" volunteers in its ranks. Bear in mind that this was before any concentrated recruiting program had begun in this area. At this time the Waffen-SS numbered 124,199 soldiers of all ranks, both active and reserve. This total would surpass the million mark, of all nationalities, by the end of the war. Of this early contingent, 583 SS soldiers were ethnic Germans from other countries and 111 were non-German volunteers of "Germanic extraction".

In May 1940 there were ten ethnic-German Britons in the Waffen-SS (three in the SS-Totenkopf Standarten and seven in the SS-Polizei Division). Eight more Englishmen of "Germanic extraction" also were serving (one in the SS-Verfügungstruppe Ersatz Bataillon, five in the SS-Totenkopf Division and two in the SS-Totenkopf Standarten). There was also an Australian ethnic-German volunteer and some South-West African volunteers; three ethnic Germans and two of "Germanic extraction".

In addition there were eight American ethnic-Germans serving in the Waffen-SS (two in the SS-Verfügungs Division and three each in the SS-Totenkopf Standarten and Division). Five other Americans of "Germanic extraction" were also in the SS-Totenkopf Division. The largest group of "Germanic extraction" volunteers at this time came from Switzerland; a total of 44 in all who served in all of the major armed SS units. The largest group of ethnic-Germans, 110 in total, came from Romania. All told, the 694 "non-Germans" in May 1940 came from about 40 different countries, including Palestine, the Dutch Indies, Mexico, China, East Africa, New Guinea, Brazil, Greece and most of the other European nations. These early volunteers were just that;

they had not been recruited but came on their own from all over the world to apply for duty in the Armed SS!

Chapter 8

The Fates of the
British Waffen-SS Volunteers

OR the first time I am able to detail what happened to some of the British Waffen-SS volunteers after the war using in nearly all cases, their correct names. There were some surprising discoveries including that of an American volunteer who served in the British Free Corps (BFC). So this will be supplemental to our earlier published material on the subject. It should be noted that many of the volunteers are not listed here as they were either tried in "secret" so as not to compromise British military intelligence, or at a later date than the ones that do appear here.

1. Frank Axon. Frank Axon was a military driver who was captured in Greece in 1941. He joined the BFC in March 1945 serving with it, and "assisting other German units" on the Eastern front for a period of six weeks. After the war he was sent to prison at hard labor until January 1948.

2. Ronald David Barker. Ronald Barker was an Australian merchant seaman captured at sea in 1941. He allegedly deserted from the BFC while en route to the Oder River Front in 1945. He was sentenced to two years at hard labor.

3. John Beckwith. John Beckwith joined the BFC in 1944 and was captured in Italy in 1945. He was sentenced to three years in prison. Beckwith made news in 1976 by attempting to get the West German government to pay him back wages and damages for the time he spent in prison!

4. Douglas Berneville-Clay. Douglas Berneville-Clay was the only known member of the "elite" British Special Air

Service (SAS), to serve in the BFC. His ultimate fate is unknown.

5. Kenneth Edward Berry. Kenneth Berry was a British merchant seaman captured in 1940. After being sent to the 11.SS-Pz.Gr.Div. "Nordland" in March 1945, he fell into Russian captivity during the unit's only battle skirmish. He received only nine months at hard labor after claiming that he had voluntarily surrendered to the Soviets.

6. Thomas Haller Cooper. The part-German Thomas Cooper was one of the senior NCOs (SS-Oberscharführer) in the BFC. He was quite active in the formation and recruitment of the unit and had been wounded in combat serving with the "Leibstandarte SS Adolf Hitler". As a result, Cooper was sentenced to death by a British military tribunal in 1945. He was given a reprieve in February 1946 when the court took into account his dual loyalties due to his German mother. Cooper was released from prison, (unrepentant!), in 1953 and promptly took off for parts unknown. An expert linguist, it is thought that in recent years he has been a foreign language instructor under an assumed identity in the Orient. In the last couple of years, the "Nazi-hunters" and the British government have been conducting a search for him as a potential "war criminal". It seems that Cooper had done some barrack room bragging about liquidating some of the "enemy" while on security duty in Poland early in the war. It is not unusual for military/police members to occasionally "spin yarns" like this for the benefit of their junior subordinates. But this was enough for the hate-mongers to jump on Cooper's case. He has now been called "Britain's Greatest Mass-Murderer" and, one of my favorite clichés, "A Cog in the Nazi Death Machine"! It is extremely unlikely that he was either of the above. Hopefully he will not be located by the "lynch mob" that is currently going after him!

7. Reginald Leslie Cornford. Reginald Cornford is thought to be the only BFC member to have been killed in action. On 27 April 1945, during the battle for Berlin, Cornford disabled a Soviet tank with a panzerfaust. The tank crew then tracked him down and shot him. Due to his unusual BFC uniform his Soldbuch (identity book) was taken and kept by a Russian officer.

8. Ray Nicholas Courlander. Courlander was a New Zealand Lance-Corporal. He served in the BFC and the SS War Reporter's Regiment "Kurt Eggers". He was captured in full BFC uniform by the British in Brussels, Belgium in September 1945 and was subsequently sentenced to fifteen years in prison.

9. Hugh Wilson Cowie. Cowie was a 27-year old military police private who enlisted in the BFC. He was later sentenced to fifteen years in prison.

10. Frederick Arthur Croft. Croft was an artillery gunner who had been captured in Libya in 1941. After making seven failed escape attempts he decided to join the BFC. He was sent to the 11.SS-Pz.Gr.Div. "Nordland" at Stettin in 1945. In January 1946 he was sentenced to six months detention, (the leniency was apparently due to his many POW escape attempts).

11. Benson Railton Metcalf Freeman. Freeman was an R.A.F. officer-pilot who joined the Waffen-SS as a POW and apparently wrote pro-German radio scripts. He was later sent to prison for ten years.

12. John Galaher. Galaher was a 24-year old member of the Canadian Essex Scottish Rgt. who had been captured at Dieppe. His trial was held in secret on "intelligence" grounds even though the war was over. He was sentenced to life in prison.

13. George Hale. Hale was an American citizen born in Vassar, Michigan. He had also been captured at Dieppe while serving with the Canadian Essex Scottish Rgt. Hale had a German grandmother and was evidently pro-German in outlook, which was why he joined the BFC. Although a

U.S. citizen in a Canadian regiment, the British later sent him to prison for ten years!

14. Dennis John Leister. Leister was a pacifist farm worker on the island of Jersey when the Germans occupied the island in 1940. After working for the occupation forces, he volunteered for the BFC in 1944. He was captured by the Americans in Italy in 1945 and was later sentenced to three years in prison.

15. Francis George McLardy. McLardy was a pharmacist from Liverpool and a Sergeant in the Royal Army Medical Corps. He was captured in 1940 and subsequently worked in a POW hospital in Poland. He later sent in a written request to enlist in the Waffen-SS to fight against Bolshevism, so there was no question about his sincerity in this regards. McLardy became one of the founding members of the "Legion of St. George"/"British Free Corps". Later on he joined the SS medical corps and helped with informational broadcasts. He was sentenced to life in prison in January 1946. McLardy was eventually released after having served 15 years in prison.

16. Edwin Martin. Martin was another member of the Canadian Essex Scottish Regiment that was captured at Dieppe. He joined the BFC in March 1944 and served as a recruit trainer. After the war he was sentenced to 25 years in prison.

17. Alfred Vivian Minchin. Minchin was another merchant seaman who became an early member of the "Legion of St. George". He claimed to instrumental in changing the unit name to the "British Free Corps". He was later sent to prison for 7 years.

18. Eric Pleasants. Erich Pleasants was probably the most colorful member of the BFC. He was born in 1911 in Norfolk and he obtained a degree in physical education and physiotherapy. He worked as a professional wrestler under the name of "Panther" Pleasants and he claimed to have been a physical trainer for members of the royal family. He also served briefly as a "security" man for the

British Union of Fascists in Norfolk. When the war with Germany came he declared himself a pacifist and he was sent to the island of Jersey to engage in farm work. After the Germans occupied Jersey, Pleasants found himself interned, so he eventually volunteered to serve in the BFC to "improve his diet" among other reasons. He then served as the "physical training" director for the BFC. While stationed at the SS Engineer School at Dresden with the other British volunteers, Pleasants began to represent the facility in boxing matches with other SS/Polizei units. In fact he later claimed to have become the "middleweight boxing champion" of the SS! He did continue to engage in exhibition matches until the last months of the war. Pleasants married a German woman and witnessed the fire bombing of Dresden from the outskirts of the city. He was able to survive the battle of Berlin and escaped from that city posing as a Wehrmacht soldier. In the process he killed two Russian soldiers in hand-to-hand combat. Pleasants than managed to escape to the American lines. He later would consider the American occupation troops to be far more brutal in their treatment of civilians than either the Russians or the Germans! When the Russians assumed the American zone in central Germany, Pleasants stayed on working as a "strongman/entertainer". Eventually the Russians became suspicious of him and felt he might be a western spy, so he was sent to the slave labor camp at Vorkuta for seven years. Thanks to his strong constitution, he managed to survive the ordeal. Pleasants later returned to England and lived in his native Norfolk until his death in 1998 at the age of 87.

19. Herbert George Rowlands. At 37 years of age, Rowlands was one of the oldest BFC members. A merchant seaman, he had been a former communist who had fought in the Spanish Civil War. He received two years at hard labor.

20. Henry Alfred Symonds. Symonds was one of the youngest BFC members, joining it at the age of 19 after having

been captured in Italy in 1943. He served the last 15 months of the war in the Waffen-SS and the vindictive court that tried him decided that he should be imprisoned one year for every month he had served in the BFC, so he was sentenced to 15 years in prison.

21. John Eric Wilson. Wilson was a British Army commando from Blackpool who was sentenced to 10 years in prison for serving in the BFC.

At least a half-dozen members of the BFC who were identified at a later date were never imprisoned but were given only a "warning". One BFC member escaped to France and was later killed by police while posing as an American soldier. At least three South African and three Australian BFC members were either never tried or never imprisoned. The "SAS" BFC member, Douglas Berneville-Clay was apparently released due to "insufficient evidence", but was later court-martialed on a trumped up charge.

Some new books have appeared concerning the BFC, including *Jackals of the Reich* by Ronald Seth (very hostile), and *Renegades: Hitler's Englishmen* by Adrian Weale (moderately hostile but informative). Earlier books concerning BFC members include *The Trial of William Joyce* (1946) by C.E. Bechhofer, which details some of the fates of the BFC members, and *I Killed to Live* (1957), which is an "as told to" autobiography of Eric Pleasants.

The former SS-Hauptsturmführer (Captain) Hans Roepke, who had commanded the Britisches Freikorps, recently summed up the unit's mission: "POWs were asked to help defend Europe against Bolshevism ... I believe that for most, they were not joining an enemy force, but were just trying to get out of camp life or wanted to fight Bolshevism. Like many thousands of volunteers from other European countries, they came to the BFC acting in good faith, and without any interest in National Socialist ideas. The sad fact that they were treated like traitors leaves a mark on those who punished them ..."

I found an obituary of Eric Pleasants, one of the more important members of the Britisches Freikorps, to be quite interesting, not only because of the personality involved but because of the fairness and quality of the writing. The same thing in a U.S. newspaper would be done in the standard hysterical hyena-hatchet job form that we have come to expect of our controlled press, with "Nazi" plastered over it and quotes from a smirking "tolerance" expert! So it is quite refreshing to see this type of reporting which appeared in a British regional newspaper, *The Eastern Daily Press* for Thursday, 30 July 1998.

Under the title of *Strong Man in War and Peace*, the obituary described Pleasants as a boxer, wrestler and strongman who was credited with "bringing Judo to Norwich". It notes that he was born in the town of Saxlingham and by the age of 15 had discovered that his "strength" and fortitude could make him money and as a result he became a professional boxer and wrestler. Among others he fought the famous Norwich boxer Ginger Sadd twice but ultimately had to switch to wrestling when his boxing injuries led to "double vision". As an amateur wrestler he was selected as a reserve to the British Olympic team at Berlin in 1936. Following this he became an instructor for young people in physical fitness and the martial arts.

The obituary mentions that his political affiliations as a Fascist for a time and later his membership in the British Free Corps, brought him some "controversy". He had been a member of the Norwich branch of the "B.U.F." (British Union of Fascists) before more or less dropping out. When the war broke out, Pleasants aligned himself with what was known as the Peace Pledge Union, a pacifist group and he went to work in the Channel Islands. According to this piece, Pleasants was arrested by the Germans for stealing petrol to fuel a boat that he was going to take back to England and was subsequently sent to a POW camp in France.

The obituary more or less skips the details about his membership in the BFC, saying that he joined basically only as method to attempt to "escape" and did not see it as an act of any "political" or "moral" significance, since he was "not fighting for anyone's flag". It then notes his postwar career as a "circus strong man" in East Germany and his endeavor to help people to escape to the Western Zone of Germany before mentioning his arrest and imprisonment in a Siberian slave labor camp in 1947 as a "spy". It then noted that Pleasants was released in a British-Soviet prisoner exchange in 1954 and that his return to his mother's home in Rackheath received newsreel coverage at the time.

Erich Pleasants then spent over 30 years as martial arts instructor in Norwich and Wymondham and did some woodcarving on the side as a hobby that he had picked up in the Soviet Siberian labor camp. Among other things he qualified as physiotherapist and masseuse in the late 1980s and taught self-defense to elderly retired people. He also had to fight back from a stroke that left him nearly paralyzed for six months and learned to speak again. His story was covered at one time in a television documentary entitled *Man of Iron*. Pleasants died on 25 July 1998. He had lived in the town of Hethel near Norwich and left a widow, Pauline. He was 87 years old at the time.

Roster of the British Free Corps of the Waffen-SS

"They fought for Britain and Europe against communism!"

1. John Amery. Founder and Leader of the Legion of St. George and the British Free Corps. Executed on December 29th, 1945 at Wandsworth Prison in London.
2. Thomas Haller Cooper. British Union of Fascists (BUF), "Leibstandarte SS Adolf Hitler" and the BFC. Sentenced to 8 years imprisonment.
3. William John Alexander. Scottish Highland Light Infantry and the BFC. Fate unknown.
4. Wilhelm August "Bob" Rossler. German BFC interpreter. Surrendered to the Soviets after running out of ammunition during the battle of Berlin, 1945. Fate unknown.
5. Roy Regan. SS-Scharführer (Sergeant) with the BFC and the SS War Reporters Regiment "Kurt Eggers". Wounded during an anti-partisan operation in Belgium, 1945. Sentenced to 15 years imprisonment.
6. Raymond Metcalfe. SS-Obersturmführer (1st Lt.) with the BFC and the SS War Reporters Regiment "Kurt Eggers". Fate unknown.
7. Anthony Wood. BFC and Waffen-SS Medical Service. Formery Royal Army Medical Corps. Surrendered to U.S. forces on the French-Belgian border in March 1945.
8. E. Durin. SS-Mann (Private). Civilian BFC volunteer from the Channel Islands. Fought against the Soviets during the last battle in Berlin. Escaped capture but ultimate fate is unknown.

9. Robert Turner. SS-Rottenführer in the BFC and medic with the 11.SS-Pz.Gr.Div. "Nordland". Destroyed a Soviet tank with a "Panzerschrek" hand-held anti-tank weapon. Wounded. Fate unknown.

10. Archibald Webster. A Lieutenant in the West Yorkshire Regiment, became an SS-Hauptsturmführer in the BFC. Returned to England after the war and retained his British Army officer's commission! Escaped prosecution.

11. "Tug" Montgomery. Became an SS-Scharführer; had been a British Army commando. Was an anti-tank training instructor for the BFC. Sentenced to 10 years at hard labor after the war.

12. SS-Hauptsturmführer "D", the German commander of the BFC. He destroyed a tank with a *"Panzerfaust"* during the battle of Berlin. Ultimate fate unknown.

13. SS-Scharführer Hodge. He led the BFC combat group in action against the Soviets at the battle of Schoeneberg in March 1945. Fate unknown.

14. Roy Ralph Futcher. Served in the Duke of Cornwall's Light Infantry and the BFC. Arrested in Germany on 3 May 1945. Cautioned, but no further prosecution.

15. Harry Dean Batchelor. Served as a sapper in the Royal Engineers and with the BFC and "Nordland" Division. Acquitted after the war due to "improper interrogation and questioning" (torture?) by British detectives.

16. Lieutenant Bissell, BFC and "senior British officer" with the so-called SS "Irish" Brigade (a conglomeration of volunteers of Irish ancestry, rather than a cohesive unit). Fate unknown.

17. John McGrath. Major of the Royal Engineers. Served with the BFC and the SS "Irish" Brigade.

18. Fred Blewitt. RAF bombardier. Was with the BFC at the Grenshagen Barracks. Fate unknown.

19. Jimmy Newcomb. BFC driver at the Grenshagen Barracks. Fate unknown.

20. Gordon Bowler. SS-Unterscharführer with the BFC. Served as a medical orderly at the Grenshagen Barracks. Captured 3 May 1945. Fate unknown.
21. Harry Blackman. Sergeant in the Essex Regiment and the BFC. Captured in Germany on 3 May 1945. Fate unknown.
22. James Brady, Royal Irish Fusiliers. His story has been recounted earlier in *Siegrunen*. He served in the BFC and the "Irish" SS Brigade. He was an SS-Unterscharführer with Otto Skorzeny's SS-Jagdverbände "Mitte", of Operation "Panzerfaust" (securing of Budapest in October 1944), fame. Wounded three times in action fighting Soviet attacks in Germany. Escaped capture until surrendering in September 1946. Subsequently jailed for 12 years.
23. Frank Stringer, Royal Irish Fusiliers. He served in the BFC and the "Irish" SS Brigade, along with at least 50 other Irish SS officers, NCOs and soldiers, Fought during the battle of Berlin. Fate unknown.
24. William Charles Britten. Lance-Corporal, Royal Warwickshire Regiment and British Army commando. Served as a tailor and supply clerk with the BFC. Fate unknown.
25. John Beckwith. Joined the BFC in 1944. Sentenced to 3 years imprisonment after the war.
26. Frank Axon. Royal Army Service Corps. Joined the BFC in March 1945. Later imprisoned at hard labor until 1948.
27. Douglas Berneville-Clay. Special Air Service (SAS) and BFC. Later court-martialed; ultimate fate unknown.
28. Kenneth Edward Berry. Merchant Navy. Joined the BFC in 1944 at the age of 19. Captured by the Soviets during the battle of Scheeneberg. Received 9 months of hard labor after being repatriated.
29. Reginald Leslie Cornford. BFC volunteer who was killed in action during the battle of Berlin on 27 April 1945 after destroying a Soviet tank with a panzerfaust.
30. Roy Nicholas Courlander. Member of the New Zealand Expeditionary Force. Lance Corporal. Served in the BFC and the SS War Reporter's Regiment "Kurt Eggers". Captured by the Allies in Brussels, Belgium in September 1945

while wearing full BFC uniform and insignia. Sentenced to 15 years in prison.

31. Hugh Wilson Cowie. Private in the Gordon Highlanders, the Corps of Military Police and the BFC. Later sentenced to 15 years penal servitude.

32. Frederick Arthur Croft. Served as a Royal Artillery gunner and in the BFC. Posted to Stettin in 1945 to fight the Soviets. Later sentenced to 6 months detention.

33. Benson Railton Metcalf Freeman. RAF officer and pilot before joining the BFC. Imprisoned for 10 years.

34. John Gordon Gallaher. Served in the Canadian Essex Scottish Regiment and the BFC. Later sentenced to life in prison(!).

35. George Hale. U.S. citizen of British and German ancestry. Served with the Canadian Essex Scottish Regiment and the BFC. Given 10 years imprisonment.

36. Dennis John Leister. From the Channel Islands and member of a populist political party in North London. Joined the BFC in 1944 and was captured in Italy by U.S. forces. Sentenced to 3 years imprisonment.

37. Francis George McLardy. Sergeant in the Royal Army Medical Corps and BFC. Formerly a member of the British Union of Fascists (BUF). Sentenced to 15 years imprisonment.

38. Edwin Barnard Martin. Member of the Canadian Essex Scottish Regiment and the BFC. Given 25 years imprisonment after the war.

39. Alfred Vivian Minchin. Merchant seaman and BFC member. Given 7 years imprisonment.

40. Eric Pleasants. British Union of Fascists "1" Squad Steward (Similar to an SA Leader) and BFC "Physical Training Officer". He was an SS middleweight boxing champion. Killed 2 Red Army soldiers during hand-to-hand fighting in Berlin, April/May 1945. Imprisoned at the Vorhuta Soviet Slave Labor Camp for 7 years. Later worked as a circus "strongman" in East Germany. Died on 26 July 1998 in Norfolk, England.

41. Herbert Geroge Rowlands. An ex-communist "International Brigades" volunteer during the Spanish Civil War. Served as a merchant seaman and in the BFC. Given 2 years at hard labor after the war.

42. Henry Alfred Symonds. Served in the Princess Louise Kensington Rifles and the BFC. Sentenced to 15 years in prison.

43. John Eric Wilson. A member of "3" Commando and the BFC. 10 years imprisonment.

44. Richard Paul Francis Maton. Served as a corporal in the "50" Commando (Middle East) and the BFC. Given 10 years imprisonment.

45. Edward Jackson. A private in the King's Own Royal Regiment and the BFC. Fate unknown.

46. Roy Walter Purdy. Sublieutenant and Junior Engineer in the Royal Navy with H.M.S. "Vandyke". A member of the "BUF", he served in the BFC and the "Kurt Eggers" Regiment. Released from post-war imprisonment in December 1954.

47. Raymond Davish Hughes. RAF Warrant Officer and air gunner, before joining the BFC. Later given 5 years penal servitude.

48. Frederick Lewis. Merchant seaman and member of the "BUF". He served as the "Camp Tailor" with the BFC; repairing uniforms and sewing on insignia. Later assigned to a "Work Commando" in Silesia. His fate remains unknown.

49. John Henry Owne Brown. A former member of the "BUF and Battery Quartermaster Sergeant in the Royal Artillery who joined the BFC. Fate unknown.

50. Alfred Browning. Served in the Argyll & Southerland Highlanders and the BFC. Fate unknown.

51. Private Chapman. BFC trooper. Captured in Germany on 3 May 1945. Fate unknown.

52. Arthur Chapple. Sergeant in the RASC (!) and the BFC. Fate unknown.

53. Charlie Chipchase. Served in the Australian Army and BFC; escaped prosecution.

54. Albert Stokes. Served in the Australian Army and BFC and also escaped prosecution.
55. Theo Ellsmore. Sergeant in the South African Army and BFC. Fate unknown.
56. "Nobby" Clark. A gunner in the Royal Artillery and BFC volunteers. Arrested on 3 May 1945 in Germany. Fate unknown.
57. George Croft. Served in the BFC and the 3.SS-Pz.Div. "Totenkopf". Fate unknown.
58. John Sommerville. Served in the BFC and the "Totenkopf" Division. Fate unknown.
59. Arthur James Cryderman. Private in the Saskatchewan Light Infantry and the BFC. Arrested on 3 May 1945 in Germany. Fate unknown.
60. Sergeant Cushing. BFC and SS "Irish Brigade" member. Fate unknown.
61. Private Walsh. BFC and SS "Irish Brigade" member. Fate unknown.
62. Private O'Brien. BFC and SS "Irish Brigade" member. Fate unknown.
63. Private Murphy. BFC and SS "Irish Brigade" member. Fate unknown.
64. Clifford Dowden. Gunner in the Royal Artillery and BFC volunteer. Fate. unknown.
65. Corporal Wood. Australian Army and BFC. Fate unknown.
66. Thomas Louis Freeman. Private in 7 Commando of Layforce and BFC trooper. Escaped prosecution.
67. Cyril Haines. Durham Light Infantry and BFC member. Arrested on 3 May 1945 in Germany. Fate unknown.
68. Private Van Heerden. South African Army, Long Range Desert Group & BFC member. Fate unknown.
69. Robert Reginald Heighes. Served in the Hampshire Regiment and as a "storesman" (supply clerk) in the BFC. He was killed during the Allied terror bombing of Dresden on 12 February 1945.

70. William How. Lance-Corporal in the Royal Military Police and BFC member. Also killed during the Dresden bombing raid.

71. Peter Andries Hendrik Labuschagne "Smith". South African Army and BFC. Escaped prosecution.

72. Robert Henry Lane. Served in the East Surrey Regiment and the BFC. Arrested in Germany on 3 May 1945 but escaped prosecution.

73. John Leigh. Private in the Lancashire Fusiliers and the BFC. Arrested on 3 May 1945 but his fate is unknown

74. Alexander MacKinnon. Lance-Corporal in the Cameron Highlanders and the BFC. Surrendered to Allied Forces along with Douglas Bemeville-Clay at Bad Kleinen, Germany in May 1945.

75. Douglas Cecil Mardon. Served in the South African Army and as an Unterscharführer (Sgt.) in the BFC. After the war he was fined 75 pounds for as the court said: "for acts held to contribute to the charge of high treason, but with no wish to damage your country."

76. Douglas Maylin. British Waffen-SS volunteer who was arrested on 3 May 1945 in Germany. Fate unknown.

77. William John Miller. Gunner in the Royal Artillery and BFC volunteer. Arrested on 3 May 1945 but escaped prosecution.

78. Charlie Munns. Scotsman who served with the Durham Light Infantry and the BFC. Fate unknown.

79. Harry Nightingale. Private in the Royal Artillery from Burnley and BFC member. Arrested in Germany on 3 May 1945. Fate unknown.

80. Tom Perkins. A Lance-Corporal in the Royal Military Police who joined the BFC. Arrested on 3 May 1945. Fate unknown.

81. Norman Rose. A Lance-Corporal in the East Surry Regiment. Later a Rottenführer in the BFC. Arrested on 3 May 1945. Fate unknown.

82. Lt.Colonel Stevenson. Officer in the South African Army and the BFC. Fate unknown.

83. Vivian Stranders. Highest ranking member of the BFC with the rank of SS-Sturmbannführer (Major). A British member of the NSDAP since 1932. He died in London in 1969.

84. Joseph Trinder. A Sergeant in the Royal Engineers who served on the BFC HQ staff. Fate unknown.

85. RAF Bombardier Marshall. He was a BFC Sergeant and cook with the BFC HQ staff. Fate unknown.

86. Maurice Tunmer (or Tumnor). A Briton of French ancestry who joined the "Legion of St. George" (earliest edition of the BFC) in 1943.

87. Edward Jordan. A Cornishman and British Army POW who joined the "Legion of St. George" and the BFC after the first enlistment rally held by John Amery at the St. Denis POW camp in France on 21 April 1943. He was later captured by the Soviets during the battle of Schoeneberg in 1945.

88. Repatriated to England, he was sentenced to 9 months in prison.

89. Kenneth Edwards. A British Waffen-SS captured by the Soviets at Schoeneberg in 1945. His fate is unknown.

90. Professor Logio. A British academic of Italian ancestry. He volunteered to join the "Legion of St. George" in 1943. His fate is unknown.

91. Laurens Viljoen. Corporal in the South African Army and BFC member. Later tried for "treason" and acquitted.

92. John Welch. Private in the Durham Light Infantry and BFC soldier. Fate unknown.

93. John Wilson. Served in the Durham Light Infantry and BFC. Fate unknown.

94. Eric Wilson. A member of the Number 3 Commando and the BFC. Arrested on 3 May 1945, but his fate is unknown.

95. Robert Henry Lane. East Surrey Regiment and the BFC. Fate unknown.

96. Tom Kipling. Gunner in the Royal Artillery and BFC member. Fate unknown.

97. Sgt. Major Own. Served as the Quartermaster Sgt. with the BFC. Fate unknown.

98. Sgt. Dixon. Senior Medical Orderly with the BFC. Fate unknown.

99. Sgt. Major Taylor. Served in the Hampshire Regiment and the BFC. Fate unknown.

100. Walter Plauen. British SS Legionnaire. Fate unknown.

101. Sgt. Edward Bartlett. BFC/W-SS NCO. Fate unknown.

102. Sgt. Miltion. BFC/W-SS NCO from the Merchant Navy. Fate unknown.

103. James Conen. A Londoner who served both in the BFC and the "Leibstandarte SS Adolf Hitler" (!). Was decorated with the Iron Cross, 2nd Class while serving on the Eastern Front. Fate unknown.

104. William J. Celliers. South West African Police and the BFC. Also decorated with the Iron Cross, 2nd Class. Fate unknown.

105. SS-Scharführer (Sgt.) Frank McCarthy. BFC NCO. Fate unknown.

106. SS-Hauptsturmführer (Captain) Harry Mehner. American of German descent. Served as the Assistant Officer Commanding of the BFC. Fate unknown.

107. Harry Davies. Private in a Parachute Regiment and the BFC. Fate unknown.

108. Reverend Jones. BFC Chaplain who served both Protestants and Catholics in the unit at the Genshagen Barracks. Fate unknown.

109. SS-Scharführer Peter Butcher (Sgt.). Served with the BFC HQ staff. Fate unknown.

110. Private Davies. One of the first BFC recruits at the age of 18. Fate unknown.

111. Godfrey Martins. A Lance Corporal in the British Army and BFC. Fate unknown.

112. Sandy Street. A Londoner from Brixton. Private. Served in the British Army and BFC. Fate unknown.

113. Walter Lander. Able Seaman. Served in the Royal Navy and BFC. Fate unknown.

114. Rudyard Meredith. BFC volunteer. Fate unknown.

115. William Bryant. Private. Served in the British Army and BFC. Fate unknown.
116. Alfred Robinson. Private. Served in the British Army and BFC. Fate unknown.
117. Arthur Tilbury. Served in the Canadian Army and the BFC. Fate unknown.
118. Buck Rogers. Served in the Canadian Army and the BFC. Fate unknown.
119. Theo Maertens. Afrikaner. Served in the South African Army and the BFC. Fate unknown.
120. Lieutenant Tyndal of the U.S. Army Air Corps. Born in Texas to an English father and German mother. He joined the BFC in early 1944. Fate unknown.
121. Private Hundrupe. BFC trooper and former "BUF" members. Fate unknown.
122. Robert Kingsely. British SS volunteer. Fate unknown.
123. Bookie Brown. Lance-Corporal in the Indian Military Police who joined the BFC. Fate unknown.
124. Charles Cameron. British SS volunteer. Fate unknown.
125. Lionel Frost. A Corporal in the British Army who joined the BFC. Fate unknown.
126. David Voysey. Served in the Australian Army and the BFC. Fate unknown.
127. Roland Miller. British SS volunteer. Fate unknown.
128. Corporal Clyde. Member of the Highland Light Infantry who joined the BFC. Fate unknown.
129. Private Nicholson. Member of the Green Howards who joined the BFC. Fate unknown.
130. Private Reeves. Member of the Duke of Cornwall Light Infantry who joined the BFC. Fate unknown.
131. Private Snell. British Army and BFC member. Fate unknown.
132. Private Thrush. Member of the Royal Artillery and the BFC. Fate unknown.
133. Private Bryant. British Army and BFC member. Fate unknown.

134. Private Giffard. British Army and BFC member. Fate unknown.
135. Private Jackson. British Army and BFC member. Fate unknown.
136. Bernard Walters. Served in the British Army and BFC. Fate unknown.
137. Private White. British Army and BFC member. Fate unknown.
138. Private Adriaan Smith. Served with the South African Army and the BFC. Fate unknown.
139. Jan Pieterson. Served with the South African Army and the BFC. Fate unknown.
140. Ian Hardcastle. Served in the British Army and the BFC. Fate unknown.
141. Lance-Corporal Culley. Member of the British Army and BFC. Fate unknown.
142. Private Atkins. British Army and BFC member. Fate unknown.
143. Private Nixon. British Army and BFC member. Fate unknown.
144. Private Sterling. British Army and BFC member Fate unknown.
145. Private Emery. British Army and BFC member. Fate unknown.
146. Private Rendsberg. Served with the South African Army and the BFC. Fate. unknown.
147. Private Reid. British Army and BFC member. Fate unknown.
148. Keith Britton. British Army Private who volunteered for the BFC. Fate unknown.
149. Private Davis. Battery Signaller who served in the BFC. Fate unknown.
150. Sandy Lane. Private in the British Army and BFC volunteer. Fate unknown.
151. Private Rogers. Served in the British Army and BFC. Fate unknown.

152. Lieutenant W.A.W. Shearer. Scottish British Army officer who served in the BFC. Fate unknown.

153. Private Frazer. Served in the South African Army and BFC. Fate unknown.

154. Ronald David Barker. A member of the Merchant Navy who joined the BFC. Sentenced to two years hard labor after the war.

155. Private Schmetterling. A British citizen of German descent who joined the BFC. Fate. unknown.

156. Private Sturmer. German volunteer of the BFC. Fate unknown.

157. Joe Philpotts. British Army Private and BFC member. Fate unknown.

158. Lance-Sgt. Harold Cole. A member of the Royal Engineers who joined the BFC. In November 1945 he escaped from a detention center in Paris dressed in an American Army uniform. He was subsequently killed in a gun battle with the French police.

159. Riflemen Carl Hoskins. A member of the K.R.R.C. (?) and BFC. Fate unknown.

160. Shaun O'Connor. An Irish volunteer of the BFC. Had been a farm worker in the Channel Islands and signed up for the BFC with Eric Pleasants after the German occupation began. Fate unknown.

161. Lieutenant-Corporal R. Spillman. Served in the K.R.R.C. and the BFC. Fate unknown.

162. Sgt. Smith. A BFC-SS NCO at the "Haus Germanen" ("Germanic House") recruit/training center for the BFC. Fate unknown.

163. Guardsman W.H. Griffiths. Served in the Welsh Guards and BFC. Fate unknown.

164. Frank Chetwynd Becker. BFC volunteer who served as an interpreter for the Free Indian Legion. Fate unknown.

165. Ernest Nicholls. A Private in the Royal Army Service Corps and the BFC. Fate unknown.

Compiler's note: Several other British and White Commonwealth volunteers saw served with the British Free Corps who so far remain unidentified.

SOURCE MATERIAL

Public Records Office. Recently released Home Office files of the British Free Corps.

Britsches Freikorps: British Volunteers of the Waffen-SS and *Siegrunen* issues Numbers 63 and 66. SR Publications, USA.

Yeoman of Valhalla by the Marquis de Slade. Mannheim, Germany, 1970.

I Killed to Live by Erich Pleasants. Great Britain, 1957.

MI5 Report on the British Free Corps, 27 March 1945.

Renegades: Hitler's Englishmen by Adreain Weale. Great Britain, 1994.

Jackals of the Reich by Ronald Seth. Great Britain, 1972.

The Trial of William Joyce by C.E. Bechofer. Great Britain, 1946.

Hitler's Englishman: The Crimes of 'Lord Haw-Haw' by Francis Selwyn. Great Britain, 1987.

Personal testimony of ex-BFC veterans.

Editor's note: The author/compiler of this piece submitted this to me anonymously. I thank him for his work and contribution of what is probably the most detailed list of British/Commonwealth volunteers ever assembled.

Epilogue

WHILE the British Free Corps could hardly be called a great success as a military unit, the very fact that it existed at all, against all of the odds, is a compliment to the unprecedented dynamism of the international Waffen-SS. Those British volunteers that did serve at least had the satisfaction of knowing that they did their share in the struggle for the values of Western Civilization, which is more than most of their fellow countrymen can say. The Allied victory established Bolshevik terror throughout much of the world for the next several decades and helped to destroy or erode almost 2,000 years of civilized progress in global history. It was in a very real sense a bleak, "hollow" victory that launched all of the European and European descended societies into a massive decline and decay that continues to this day.

The fact that the British SS volunteers fought against this darkness will be to their eternal credit. Whenever the true history of the 20th Century is written in some future era, their contributions, however slight in the grand scheme of affairs, will be rightfully honored. And the actions of their countrymen and the other Allies who helped bring about the New Dark Ages, will most certainly be scorned.

Bibliography

The Allgemeine SS (S.H.A.E.F. Handbook), 1945.

Angolia, LTC (Ret.) John R. *Cloth Insignia of the SS*. San Jose: Bender Publishing, 1983.

Beadle, C. and Hartmann, T. *The Waffen-SS: Its Divisional Insignia*. England: Key Publications, 1971.

Bender, R.J. and Taylor, H.P. *Uniforms, Organization and History of the Waffen-SS, Vol. 2*. Mountain View: Bender Pub., 1972.

Buss, Philip H. and Mollo, Andrew. *Hitler's Germanic Legions*. London: MacDonalds and Janes, 1978.

de Slade, Marquis, *Yeomen of Valhalla*. Mannheim, Germany, 1970 (?).

Gefaehrten Unsrer Jugend. Germany: Verlag K.W. Schuetz, 1984.

Klietmann, Dr. K.-G., *Die Waffen-SS: Eine Dokumentation*. Germany: Verlag "Der Freiwillige, 1965.

Landwehr, Richard. "The Saga and Ordeal of the British Free Corps." *Siegrunen Bulletin*, 1980.

Littlejohn, David, *Foreign Legions of the Third Reich, Vol. 2*. San Jose: Bender Pub., 1981.

Mabire, Jean. *Berlin im Todeskampf 1945*. Germany: Verlag K.W. Schuetz, 1977.

—. *Die SS-Panzer-Division Viking*. Germany: Verlag K.W. Schuetz, 1983.

—. *La Division Nordland*. France: Fayard, 1982.

Neulen, Hans Werner. *An Deutscher Seite*. Munich: Universitas Verlag, 1985.

Pioniere der Waffen-SS im Bild. Germany: Munin Verlag, 1985.

Quarrie, Bruce. *Hitler's Samurai* (2nd Edition). England: Patrick Stevens, Ltd., 1984.

Taylor, Hugh Page. *Uniforms of the SS, Vol. 2: Germanische-SS, 1940-45*. London: Historical Research Unit, 1969.

West, Rebecca. *The New Meaning of Treason*. New York: Time, Inc., 1966.

Notes on Sources

THE definitive "history" to date of the BFC has to be *Yeoman of Valhalla* by de Slade. Although hard to read, sarcastic and somewhat bizarre in content, this privately printed volume is filled with "inside information". It is also basically non-hostile to the subject. *Die Waffen-SS: Eine Dokumentation* by Klietmann remains the best one-volume study of the Waffen-SS ever attempted; its coverage of the BFC is concise and accurate. *The New Meaning of Treason*, although basically a leftist "tract", devotes a good deal of space to several members of the BFC. It is viciously hostile to the British volunteers. Good BFC photos can be found in *Foreign Legions of the Third Reich, Vol. 2* and *Hitler's Samurai* (2nd Edition). From the point of view of text, both of these titles are extremely flawed. *Gefaehrten Unsrer Jugend* contains an extremely detailed account of the Britons in service with the "Leibstandarte" and takes a very positive view of the British volunteers.

The skirmish at Schoeneberg is recounted in *The New Meaning of Treason* but not in *Yeomen of Valhalla*. But it still seems to have taken place as a Free Corpsman was captured by the Soviets there. Littlejohn, in *Foreign Legions, Vol. 2*, states that two BFC members were killed in the fire-bombing of Dresden. Since I have not seen this mentioned elsewhere it was left out of the text, although it may well have happened. The individual in the photo on page 58 has been identified as a BFC deserter by de Slade. Apparently the picture appeared as part of a propaganda article in a Norwegian pro-Axis newspaper, and perhaps elsewhere in other Axis publications. Much of the story of the BFC remains unverified and is likely to remain so and most of the writing on the subject has been hostile and sarcastic. I have endeavored to reverse that trend, hopefully with some success!

Printed in Great Britain
by Amazon

58041252R00059